D1304892

I WANT IT NOW!

I WANT IT NOW!

Analyze Where You Are in Life
Discover Your PASSION and
Achieve Ultimate Happiness

Na'Kisha Crawford, M.Ed

Pathway Publishing
Rancho Cucamonga, CA

Pathway Publishing
9849 Foothill Blvd. Suite A
Rancho Cucamonga, CA 91730

Copyright © 2003 by Na'Kisha Crawford

All Rights Reserved. This book may not be reproduced in whole or in part, stored in a retrieval system, or transmitted in any form or by any means electronic, mechanical, or other without written permission from the publisher, except by a reviewer, who may quote brief passages in a review.

Cover & Interior Design: Irene Archer, www.book-cover-design.com
Edited by: Michael McIrvin, /mcirvinm@earthlink.net

Publisher's Cataloging-in-Publication
(Provided by Quality Books, Inc.)

Crawford, Na'Kisha.
I Want it Now!: Analyze Where You are in Life,
Discover Your Passion and Achieve Ultimate Happiness /
Na'Kisha Crawford.
p. cm.
LCCN: 2003096066
ISBN: 0-9744769-0-0

1. Success. 2. Happiness. 3. Self-management (Psychology)
4. Quality of life. 5. Personality and occupation. I. Title.

BF637.S8C73 2004   158.1
QBI03-700728

No one thinks that one person
could make a great change
but at the bottom of a great change
is the thought of one person
so dream what you want to dream.

CONTENTS

I close my eyes and I think of
all the things that I want to see
Now that I've opened up my heart
*I know that **Anything I want can be.***

—*India Arie*

Acknowledgements

I would first like to acknowledge and thank The Creator for having this fabulous plan for my life, for opening my heart and my eyes to the vision and for leading me to it. Life is for living with joy and abundance. Thank you.

To my husband, my soul mate and strongest supporter, Mr. LaRon Hall, you are my joy. You give unselfishly and you would not let me fail. I love you so much for believing in me and for always staying by my side. Thank you, Baby.

To my Spiritual Advisor, G. Michael Smith, I thank you for your kind words of support and guidance as well as your warming smile.

Mom and Dad, I love and appreciate you both. You gave it to me and now I am working so hard to give it back. Mom, Glory Williams, you have taught me how to overcome adversity and to do it with a smile on my face and my hands on my hips. Dad, Albert Crawford, your undying love for and belief in me has tricked me into thinking that I can do just about anything. Thank you. My grandparents, Dee and Jay (both deceased) were and Nora Mae is absolutely wonderful.

My brothers and sisters, I love you guys. Thanks for being in my corner no matter which way I chose and thanks for understanding me even when you did not. My family is amazing. You have never met a more interesting bunch of people which would explain why once someone came around us, they never wanted to leave. We have undoubtedly had our share of problems but I have learned so much about life through your experiences.

My best friends are so special to me as I expressed to each of you personally on August 30, 2002. To my sorors of Delta Sigma Theta Sorority, Inc. especially Eta Omega Chapter and Six Degrees of Determination, you have all been such a blessing. I have learned some of life's toughest lessons and enjoyed some of life's best times with you. Thank you.

I have really had a lot of great support over the years and I acknowledge and thank all of you. It is very important to me that I acknowledge those of you that I have motivated because you keep me inspired. Thank you.

For those of you that helped me to turn this vision and dream into reality, I thank you.

INTRODUCTION

I was once told to jump in there and let it flow when I had something to say that I felt was important, so here it is. I am very passionate about the things that I feel, and I want to share with readers the things that I have learned. Which brings me to the point, why I wrote a book about my experiences and the real life lessons that I have learned.

I enjoy sharing with and helping others, and I have always known that my occupation would somehow involve those things. As a young person, most of us have a hard time determining what we are going to be in life, and in fact, we find that a tough decision to make even as mature adults. Our hobbies or the specifics of how we spend our spare time may change in life as we become more experienced, cultured, or knowledgeable, but our passions remain a core part of who we are, of our identity. I have always been passionate about helping others, and this book is an expression of that core passion that makes me who I am.

It is my goal to inspire and motivate others. I want people to find what makes them happy in life, to find their passions. Life challenges each of us with experiences and lessons that, if we share them with others, will make the same or like experiences for others just a bit less challenging, a bit less harrowing perhaps. Discovering those things that make you feel good is a learning game, but getting to the point where you can accept both those things that are enjoyable along with those that are not so much fun as a natural part of life is a bigger objective for our learning. Many people believe that life is going to be hard regardless, so when something feels too good, they believe something has to be wrong. The truth of the matter is that life is indeed hard, but the truth is also that time keeps ticking. We can either accept that having hard times means that there is no room for personal growth and development or for improvement in our selves and our lives, or we can seek to find all of the wonderful things in the world that make us happy while learning from our harsher experiences.

I share my beliefs and experiences to, hopefully, inspire you. My plan is to offer you some suggestions to get started on working toward your goals, and per-haps to help some of you get back on track and stay there. I want people to identify their professional and personal goals, or to revisit them as the case may be, and to have the confidence to step out on faith and to make changes in their lives. Some of us have become overwhelmed because we have been so busy taking on other people's problems that we have for-

gotten about our goals, for example. For such readers, it is time to figure out how to put yourself back
into the equation.

Some people wonder if they should take chances
now or wait for those life-altering experiences to land
in their laps, while many others are working to see
how far their chosen careers will take them. Now is
the time to evaluate where you are in life, discover
what you want and go out and get it. It is time to
start working on your personal journey toward ultimate happiness, to put yourself back into the equation, and to seek others who support your interest in
personal growth and development.

1st
PART OF THE PLAN

I

GET TO KNOW ME

In life, be sure that you take the time to get to know yourself. No other person is more important for you to acknowledge and understand than you. Acknowledge those experiences in life, the good and the bad, that have made you into the person you are so that you will recognize progress and growth.

Before this moment, I have never spent so much time thinking about the things that I would like others to know about me. I am usually a very open, very uninhibited person, but I realize that there are certain things that I just let others assume about the type of life that I have led. So, here are the facts, and let's start with change right from the beginning: I was born and raised in Oakland, California, until my parents decided to move to Modesto, California, which is about an hour away. At that time, I thought it was the worst thing that could have happened, but it was not long before I became grateful for that transition.

Until about the eighth grade, which was the point in my life when I moved to Modesto, I thought that the entire world was like Oakland. A big city, urban America, is what I came to love as my home. Although drugs and violence plagued many of our communities, there was always a bright side. I was still a child, but I was old enough to understand what was going on around me. I came from a very close-knit family (including my extended family), which was the beginning of so many life lessons for me. In fact, I have come to understand many of my child-hood experiences as lessons since becoming an adult, and I wish that I could point out precisely what those lessons were to the same people who unknowingly taught them to me.

In many cases, my family has taught me what not to do, and I believe that this is valuable. In fact, they have provided me with examples in some cases, step by step, of what not to do. However, the funny thing is that no one has ever pointed out to me that they were doing something that I should not, but results alone speak louder than words. I have watched several people, including my own family members, struggle with drug and alcohol abuse, violence, single parenting, unemployment, lack of education, and being poor; but we still managed to make life fun from time to time.

More intriguing to me, however, is the fact that I have watched so many of my generation fall into the same category that our parents fell into, which baffles my mind. I grew up very close to my mother's family. Everyone was young and fun, including my grandmother, who also happens to be one of the strongest women I know.

Most of my mom's family lived in the Oakland area. We celebrated just about every holiday together, but sometimes we encouraged the wrong types of activity and behavior. The saddest thing about this situation was that no one knew any better. There was really no guidance and several examples of the wrong things to do, the wrong ways to act. Unfortunately, no one realized that they were setting themselves up to fail. The things that were going on in my family were part of what was going on in Oakland.

A few years after I left, many of the girls that I hung out with had dropped out of school. Too many had gotten caught up in a lifestyle that would be the death of their dreams. Some had gotten pregnant, while others had begun to use drugs or to date drug dealers, who provided them with both a means to self-destruct and the cash that required that they do nothing else. In fact, only a couple of them were still in school, and because the local public school system was steadily deteriorating, some were being graded solely on attendance. I feel very fortunate to have left when I did, and I thank God and my parents for my escape.

Although I moved from Oakland, however, I would not escape some of the factors that shaped who I was. My family and I continued to be met by many of the same social problems that still plague our inner cities today. Money and unemployment were factors, and drugs, alcohol, and violence had not gone away just because we had moved to a new locale. I had a lot to carry as a child, but I never let these factors steal my spirit. I can not explain why I was able to break so many of the cycles that I had grown up around and within, but I do know that God carried me those times that I could not walk.

I went on to do great in school, and in fact, I liked school and never really got into too much trouble. I liked most of my teachers, and I liked participating in class. I learned to be outspoken fairly early, and I am really glad that I did speak up even though it sometimes got me into trouble. I enjoyed sports, and all in all, I was pretty involved in all of the right things. My parents were always very proud of me, and I always expected to get the most out of life. I never remember dreaming about what I was going to be when I got older, but I always knew that I would be successful. I still feel today that I am going to reach success beyond the stars. I just know that God has this place for me.

I went to college at San Jose State University in San Jose, California, where I had a blast. It was there that I came into being. I was challenged on so many levels, met some wonderful people, and learned who

I was, indeed who I am. I grew as a young woman and a scholar. I did all of the things that I wanted to do, and I have very few regrets. I have always thought that it was important not to have many regrets, so I did the things that I wanted to do, the things that I thought were best for me at the time. I majored in Sociology and graduated with honors in 1996, after just four years. After taking time off from my education for one year, I returned and earned a Master's Degree in Education, Counseling in 1999.

I went on to be the first in my family on my mother's side to graduate from college, and the first to earn a Master's Degree on either side of the family as well. I was very proud of myself, and my family was overjoyed. I attribute much of my success to them because their experiences taught me so much about life. I was happy to be up there serving as proof that it could happen for all of those who were to come after me; but perhaps even more than this, I felt an obligation to my ancestors, women, and others who had experienced similar lifestyles, for so many of them were denied the opportunity to become educated. Most importantly, I learned what it means to persevere.

I am at a point in my life now where it is extremely important to achieve my passion. Since my Master's is in Education, many will assume that I wanted to be a teacher or something like that, but I would have to answer honestly with a "not really." Let me back up and clarify that I am not interested in being a school teacher, not a teacher in the traditional sense, but my dream is to teach others how to determine what they want and how to reach their passions. I have always thought that at some point in my life I would be a good school teacher though, maybe post-secondary, after I become more patient and experienced. I am a firm believer that you should work to find those things that you love in life, those things that are important to you, and this is what I am doing for myself.

I know that in the end my life will make perfect sense. I do not have all of the answers, but I am not going to wait until I do before I make my life work. The totality of my life will come together, all of the pieces fitting together like a puzzle. Those things that I never understood will become clear, and those things that I have never been able to see will appear before me. That is the way that I expect life to turn out for me, and I believe that it is God's plan. I believe that He has this plan for all of us, if we believe in him. Have faith, and your experiences will come together to lead you in the direction of your dreams.

Exercise
Get to Know You

Write the appropriate number next to each category.

1—Not Satisfied
2—Somewhat Satisfied
3—Satisfied
4—Very Satisfied

Categories:

- Career/Job   _____
- Love Relationship   _____
- Physical Appearance   _____
- Spirituality/Religion   _____
- Social Life   _____
- Financial Status   _____
- Family Life   _____
- Car/Mode of Transportation   _____
- Living Situation   _____
- Education Level   _____
- Political Awareness & Involvement   _____
- Community Involvement   _____
- Economic Awareness   _____
- International Awareness   _____
- Computer Literacy   _____

If you selected Item 1-2 for any of the above categories, write down 3 steps that you can take to move them to a level of satisfaction.

2

DREAMER

Never give up on your dreams, and always believe in your ability to achieve personal success. Be sure to evaluate yourself because only you can develop the criteria for your peace of mind.

I am what I call a Dreamer. It is great to dream, and I enjoy it because dreaming allows me to go places, to have experiences, that may never actually become my reality. A dream can make you happy, even if only for the short time period that you are thinking about it. I am also a Believer, however, which means that I believe in my ability to make those dreams into a reality. Ever since I was a little girl, I have always known that I was supposed to be special and successful. Some of the time though, I wrote it off as every little girl's dream. But now that I am an adult, I still have that same feeling.

One thing about me is that I never believed an opportunity would just fall into my lap. I have always known that I had to work hard to make opportunities for myself. To this day, I am looking for the chance to realize my full potential. I want to be happy. I want to help others. I want to be sought out for my opinions and my advice. I want to be heard.

Personally, I have started to hear someone loud and clear, and although everyone finds that special message to do one thing or another at some time in their life, I believe the message is coming through for me to be myself. The best part about that is that I love me and I love what I do, even though I have plenty of things to work on. If you have not recognized that you have things to work on, you are not growing.

When I say that the message is to be myself, I mean that I am getting the support and the spiritual guidance to talk to others and encourage them, to be outgoing and to continue to be passionate about things of interest to me. More importantly, I am being guided to share with people some of the important lessons in my life. In fact, I feel that I am being guided to recognize the work that I do naturally, and to recognize it as intended, as part of the plan. Consequently, I am able to work without working.

I mentioned that I am getting the spiritual guidance to do what feels natural in an effort to share with you, not to throw you off course in any way. Some people get offended when something has a religious or spiritual connotation; however, it is my goal to be as honest as possible. When I refer to spiritual guidance, I am referring to something that I feel within me that provides direction and support from a greater being, something that I recognize as, and therefore name as, spiritual.

Sometimes, things begin to make sense to us, things that we have been unable to understand. It is like that lesson Mom has been repeating over and over just clicks one day and becomes perfectly clear. Sometimes, we simply begin to see things clearly that have been clouding our view. Sometimes, however, we are able to hear a voice within us, and we not only hear it, we listen. I believe that when this occurs the message comes from a greater source, a power that knows me, and I associate this connection with God, who actually lives within me. I believe that God wants love, happiness, and abundance for me in my life, and for this reason, I will achieve that love, happiness, and abundance.

When you have a positive spirit, positive things happen for you. Moreover, when you have a positive spirit, others associate you with good things. Sometimes we do something, perhaps something as simple as reading a book, and we have no idea why we decided to pick that particular something, that particular book. That book you thought you had picked up for no reason at all may force you to think about something that you have been avoiding in your life, or the simple task of reading a few pages on that day may help you to feel accomplished. It could be that you have not felt validated lately, and now that major project that you finished last week makes you feel important. Maybe today you just happened to catch a movie on television that inspired you to do something you would not have felt confident enough to do otherwise. You might also find that even though you did not share your feelings of despair with anyone, you now feel like you can climb any mountain, and it is then that you realize that it may be due to a higher power, like a spiritual connection.

I have been a pretty honest person about my feelings, which lets you know that I am a very feeling person. Though I am considerate of other people's feelings, however, my eyes sometimes tell a different story than my mouth. I have been blessed with being very expressive and very opinionated too. Yes, I said that being opinionated is a blessing because there is nothing worse than having no opinion. Trouble certainly comes when you use your opinion to place judgment on others, but no opinion at all is like being dead as far as I am concerned. However, although I find it difficult to relate to those who generally do not share their opinions as well as those who are not expressive, I am not really saying that these traits are bad, but simply that it is hard for me to relate to such a person or to this way of being in the world. It is like being at a concert with a friend who does not budge when your favorite song comes on. That is so hard for me.

I have been learning so much about myself of late that some days I am happy, some days I am sad, and other days I am just plain confused. I am a very strong person, but I am very sensitive too. I do not always remember how strong I am and whine like anyone else, but when I look back I recognize the growth, the progress that I have made, and I remember that I am very strong. In fact, I do not believe that there is true life without growth. If one is not learning new things, or even acknowledging things that have been there all along, they are not progressing. If I am not progressing, I am not living.

I am happy when I have the opportunity to make others understand something that I have grown to see so clearly. I am excited when others are motivated by my words or actions. I feel good when others can be inspired to do something that makes them feel good based upon something that I have shared with them. It is not my goal in life to push my views onto others, but I would like to help people understand those things in their own lives that help to form their views.

I am seeking to be fulfilled. I have tried a lot of things, and I always come back to the same core ideas. I am a talented person, by which I mean that I have some natural skills, things I can do because I am me. Even though I went to college and got better at a few things, I have not always realized what I was really working on. The things that I enjoy most have existed all along, and now it is important for me to share a story that others can relate to. I want you to see the visions that I am seeing so that you recognize those same signs as they keep appearing at your front door. I want you all to acknowledge your blessings as I am learning to acknowledge mine.

Over and over again, I have thought about what it is that I want to do with my life in order to feel complete. To answer this question, I have had to ask the most important question that a person can ask him or herself: What do I want? Most people spend their whole lives worrying about what they do not want instead of what they do want. Try turning that around and discovering the answer to that question in your life. Interestingly, you will find that same answer that has been there all along, that thing that you have been ignoring or covering up, that thing that makes you feel.

Exercise
Don't Be Afraid to Dream

Stop everything for a moment and think about your dream life. Get out a piece of paper and Write.

- Without thinking of why or how, the judgment that might be placed upon you or the reality and without being afraid or even knowledgeable, think about your desires. Take a moment to suspend any negative thoughts, close your eyes, and dream. What are you doing if you had everything you wanted? What is your life like? Where do you live? How much money do you have in the bank? What are your assets? How many children do you have? How do you spend your time? What is your career?

- List anything else that would be available to you in your perfect life. Do not think too hard and don't make any corrections. You can have anything you want. Now, write.

3

LIFE LESSONS
AND OPPORTUNITIES

Accept that some days are going to be exciting and that others will be more somber. Spend as much time as possible enjoying all your days, but acknowledge when you are being given the time to reflect.

The most powerful lessons in life come from the most challenging experiences, so why is it so difficult to deal with the things that teach us the most? Why is it so difficult to discover what we want out of life? Most people are afraid of what they do not know, and in many cases, what we think we want has never been our reality and thus there is much we can't know about these proposed circumstances. Consequently, we do not really even know if we should want those things because we do not want

the judgment that might follow. Also, we are sometimes unsure what will result if we are honest about
our desires because others may not be supportive. In
order to get what you want, you must speak it, see
yourself with it, and you have to accept why you want
it.

Most of us want more from life than we have,
which is really the best part of life, the desire.
Imagine having everything you want and no desires.
Imagine life without taking chances. Most of us take
chances because we want to change our circumstances or we want a better life. We spend our lifetime setting goals and working to reach them. If we
did not aspire to have more than we already have,
then life would be boring. Even those who seem to
have everything would become bored if they had
nothing to work for. In fact, however, those people
who seem to have everything, or as close to it as is
possible, either want other things most of us can't
imagine, whatever remains that they do not have, or
they are working hard to keep what they do have.
Either way, whether hungering for something new
or struggling to hold onto what one has, the key is
work.

Life does not always work out in patterns the
way so many of us feel it should, and in fact, it is usually made up of twists and turns, ups and downs. The
thing that makes any given life so unique perhaps is
that you never know when these twists may occur,
when they may happen to you or your loved ones.

Life teaches us that, regardless of how good a person you are or even how bad you are, you will experience things that you are unable to define or understand. We also learn that both good and bad things will happen and that it is all just a part of the larger plan.

In short, good things sometimes happen to bad people and bad things to good people, but I am a firm believer that there is something good to be learned from every bad experience. Sometimes we are tested in order to learn of our strength, and other times we are reminded of how good life can be if only we offer it a chance. I do not know if anyone ever knows why things really happen, but our experiences sometimes force us to take a deeper look at our situation.

I have learned something very significant in my life regarding intentions and blessings. They go hand in hand. When you have good intentions in life, and you work to see them come through in certain situations, you can watch your blessings add up. If you know something good in life, something that may help another's journey to be a little easier, it is worth sharing. Think about how many times you have been in a difficult situation and how much easier it could have been if only there were someone to share with you the possible results ahead of time.

So many good things have happened in my life that I know I am truly blessed. I have also experienced so many bad things that I know I must be blessed if I can still see life the way that I do. We all have this gift, of perseverance and being equipped to handle what confronts us — everything we need in our lives is within us. My Spiritual Advisor and friend once shared with me that, if you eat a cherry, you will find a seed inside, and if you plant that seed in the right environment, sprinkle it with a little water and nurturance, it will eventually grow into a cherry again. The seed has everything it needs inside to grow again, to become a thriving fruit-bearing tree, and the same is true for people. We all have the ability to think for ourselves and the freedom to believe what we want to believe. There is no gift greater than freedom. With this, we have control over how we feel. That is, we have control over what we allow to make us happy or make us sad. We have the freedom to care for and about whatever we like, and most importantly perhaps, we have the freedom to dream.

A life filled with dreams is a life full of possibilities. There is nothing more precious than *what could be*. Many of us reach that place in life that we have strived to get to, but it is a place for which others are constantly striving. Personally, I live my life by the belief that, as long as I strive, there is life yet unlived, goals to be reached, new experiences to be experienced. What fun would life be if there was nothing left to experience? Once a person thinks that they have done it all or that they know it all, they have stopped growing. If you are not growing, you are not living. Without expansion, there is no life.

We are born to others with certain genes and characteristics that are not determined by us, but what we do after we are born is determined by the choices we make for ourselves. However, it is also true that our environment has a great deal to do with the choices we make because most of us repeat what we have seen and learned. It is a lot easier to do what others have done before you than it is to lay a new foundation or try something new. People who do new things are often considered pioneers, and they will either be admired or despised for trying to change the status quo. It takes a remarkable person to break the cycles to which and within which they have been born, and in most cases these people are working against all odds to make things change. It has been said that there is strength in numbers, but it takes an incredible amount of strength to stand alone. I have been so inspired by something that I learned in college: no one thinks that one person can make a great change, but at the bottom of a great change is the thought of one person. This just reaffirms that you can achieve wonderful things if you believe in yourself.

I see people all of the time who I think could benefit from something that I have learned or experienced, or maybe my desire is simply to help them — and of course I believe that I could help them. I have learned so many things in my life, and the lessons have been from both good and bad experiences. I should have been learning from those experiences all along, but I have not always been alert enough to recognize them for what they were: lessons. I know that life has only begun to teach me, and I know that as long as I am willing and open to learning from my experiences, I will be blessed with the ability to share with others. The ability to share is what life has given me to be happy. Incidents only become lessons once you have learned from them, and in order for you to learn from them, you have to reflect upon your experiences.

As I stated before, it has been important for me to go through life without having any regrets. I know that not all things that happen to me will be the best for me, but I think that I stand to learn something from all of my experiences. I have tried to take my time and to think things through before making all of the important decisions in my life, and although there may have been times when I did not make the best decision, I have been able to stand by the ones that I made because of the investment that went into them. We are all expected to make some wrong choices in life, but if we choose not to learn from the bad ones, then nothing has been gained.

Life has met most of us with challenges at some point in time. If we were not challenged, however, we would never know our potential. In many cases, our greatest potential has only been realized when we were faced with adversity. Think back to one of your most challenging experiences. You probably felt like you would not get through it, but with strength and time, it passed. One of the only absolutely certain things about life is that it keeps on going whether times are good or bad. It is my goal to have as many good times as possible, but I know that the good times would be hard to recognize if there were no bad times with which to compare them.

Each of us has to decide how to handle difficult situations in life. We are not judged on what we decide, but on how we handle the decisions we make. It is important to remember that there are consequences for every action taken, and in fact, it must also be remembered that there are consequences for actions not taken as well.

It is important to find peace within regarding those difficult situations you face. There will always be bad times or difficult decisions to make, but never forget that there are always going to be others who are not at peace with your decisions and consequently we must be satisfied that we have made the best possible decision we could make. However, the more important thing for each of us to remember is that there is only one you. Everybody has the right to make decisions for themselves, and those decisions should be the best ones possible for you. I am not saying that you should not consider others in your decision making processes, but ultimately, each person has to live with and for him or herself. So, learn how to make peace with yourself first. If you decide that you must put another person's feelings or issues before your own in a particular instance, then make sure that you can be at peace with that when all is said and done. Any decision has to be one that you can live with.

Life is like a game that is never ending. We each get a stack of cards and we choose the ones that we are going to play; however, we do not choose the ones we are dealt. As with any game, we only know what we have in our own hands, and in some cases, we do not find out what is at the bottom of our stack until we get there. Life offers each of us opportunity after opportunity to practice the game, however, but rather than improve, because we are creatures of habit, many of us make mistake after mistake. We make the same choices in similar situations, which leave us with the same or similar problems.

Some people practice living until they recognize a clear vision, and others play life without thinking of a strategy at all. Some have an idea from very early on what they want in life and how they want their lives to be, but others just run into one obstacle after another — sometimes realizing that part of the bigger plan will come from these experiences and other times having no clue. The way we confront or cope with the problems that come up, the obstacles that get in our path, help to determine the types of problems we will continue to face. Do not be afraid to accept your experiences as lessons to be learned. Take time to reflect on every decision you make, good or bad, and determine how that choice has helped you to grow.

Exercise
Explore Life's Lessons

Follow the instructions provided below.

List 5 of your most difficult life experiences.

1.

2.

3.

4.

5.

How did you feel when you were confronted by each situation?

1.

2.

3.

4.

5.

What did you do to overcome this adversity?

1.

2.

3.

4.

5.

What did you learn about life from each of the above experiences that could be shared with someone who may be confronting a similar problem?

1.

2.

3.

4.

5.

2nd

PART OF THE PLAN

4

Vision and Change

*No matter what decisions you make in life, be sure
to acknowledge that God has a vision for you, and
no matter how hard you work on creating your own,
God's plan for your life will reign supreme. Spend
your time trying to align your vision with God's,
and the only way to do that is to be at peace with
your spirit. You must believe in and love yourself,
which comes as you begin to love that peace felt
when your spirit guides you.*

On life's path, you must understand that not
every person you meet can see your vision.
The truth is that most of us do not even see
our own vision clearly for ourselves, and when we do,
only parts of it can be seen with any clarity. Keep in
mind that not every person should see your vision,

which is why we are all blessed with individuality and imagination: we are all different and different visions occur and appeal to different people. Each one of us has the right to create his or her own path, just as we have the chance to work toward it.

There will always be someone out there who will speak against your vision because they cannot see it, but some people may even speak against you because they wish that your vision was their own. Without realizing it, we are very influential as human beings, but we can also be discouraged or distracted when others speak ill of us, of our lives. It is very easy to be caught off guard or knocked off track when others do not support us, especially those whom we love, which can indeed be discouraging. Only you can place a value on your plan for great things for yourself, and you also have to clarify both the plan and the value for yourself. That process alone is work. In fact, it requires dedication and a connection to your inner self.

As we discussed in the previous chapter, most of us have learned to accept that everything in life happens for a reason. In many cases, a few years may go by before we understand why something happened, or indeed we may never understand. In other words, we sometimes have to accept that things are going to happen for reasons that are sometimes bigger than us, which is just a part of accepting life. Most of us would like to go through life with as few problems as possible, but because we have lived for as long as we have, we know that life produces changes that may bring about problems.

Life should be equal to progress — the very same thing — which is a part of change, and one can not expect change without having to make any adjustments in one's life. Adjustments are the results of change, and when things do not change, there is no need to adjust. When things do go wrong, try to resolve the problems by changing something about the situation, or else you can merely live with it.

No one has a life filled with only positive experiences. It is important that we have positive wishes for others, especially for our loved ones and their issues, because another person's problems can affect our own happiness. Although many of us tell ourselves that we are not going to allow someone else's situation to make us unhappy, we live in a world populated with other people. Love between people makes the world go around. How comfortably could you rest knowing that a loved one was in a painful situation? Again, another person's situation can affect yours.

Imagine life with no one to share the good and bad times with. Since we all know that everyone experiences both positive and negative events, we should remember that someone who cares for us may also be brought down by our hard times. Think of the happiest, most successful person you know, or even know of, and you probably also know of some very hard times that person has experienced in his or her own life before things got better. This should confirm for us that no one is promised only bright days. We also have to remember that fact because we are free to make our own choices and we are in control of how we allow ourselves to feel.

No matter what happens, we have to keep a positive outlook on life. Those of us who are fortunate are able to be in the company of positive people who are realistic yet optimistic. As I mentioned before, a wonderful part about life is that we are free to dream, and the great thing about dreaming is that nothing has to make perfect sense. A positive person will support you and your dream because there are no limits to what a person can want. As long as you desire to have greater things or to be in a better place, there is always the possibility that you may get there. If you dream about it long enough, you may figure out a way to start to make it into a reality. If it never turns into a reality, you can still think of the wonderful time you had exploring the possibility or how nice it was to feel like this imagined situation could be. Life is never more special than its possibilities.

Close your eyes and think about something good (a dream) and stay there for a minute. Let your imagination run free with the possibilities. By the time you let reality back in, you are happy. Whether you dreamt for thirty minutes or three, just think of how good you felt for that period of time when what you could imagine was possible. There is probably no better feeling than obtaining your goals, and dreaming that achievement is one way to do so — and a way to begin the process of making the dream a reality.

Sometimes we find ourselves traveling in circles of people who limit us. However, it is not always apparent that, if we feel discouraged, it could be related to those with whom we have surrounded ourselves. In most cases, those that we are associated with have the greatest effect on what we see ourselves doing. Sometimes, people carry a negative energy and they do not even realize it. Some will kill your dreams as long as you share anything of yourself with them. No one wants to be around negative people, and no one usually wants to see themselves as that negative person. Worse, it may be hard to get away from the negativity because it could be a parent, sister or brother, or even your close friend, but it is best to recognize that negative energy for what it is.

Sometimes, the people who care the most about you may discourage you the most too, but they do not always realize their impact. You have to cut your ties to anything, or indeed to anyone, that hinders your growth on any level when you are trying to progress. If it happens to be a family member or close friend, at the very least limit the amount of time you spend sharing with that person. Negative people may not want to see good things happen for you, but they do not usually believe that good things can happen for themselves either, which may be the only source for their bleak outlook toward you.

I have lots of friends, and I am a much closer to some than others. Like most people, those with whom I enjoy sharing the most are those with whom I have the most in common. I dislike being around negative people: those who fail to see the light in any situation, those who refuse to be supportive. It seems that these are the same folks who are always going through a hard time but have no idea why. I tell those optimistic folks to cut the negative out of their lives, and I tell those who are pessimistic to try changing the negative thoughts to positive ones. It has been said before that you get negative results if you speak in the negative. We all know that there are two sides to every coin, however, so while I recommend cutting your ties with negative people, do not avoid those who are positive, those who actually inspire you.

Other people can be your demise, but other people can also lead you to light. We could all learn from another person's mistakes, but most of us would rather not. It never ceases to amaze me that the answers to our questions are sometimes staring us in the face, but if we did not experience a situation for ourselves, then we do not truly know the answer. Some people have to walk into the fire and get burned before they believe that, no matter who you are, fire does burn.

I am not saying that all situations will turn out

the same for every person, because they will not; but sometimes, the trouble you could save yourself is well worth the time spent listening to someone's advice. Some lessons are worth learning for ourselves, however, because often times, the more you experience something the more real it becomes to you. When things become real to you, become a part of your life, the lesson is truly learned. Once you acknowledge life's lessons, you can learn to fully appreciate life.

Often, when people advise us on how to handle situations or how to prepare for them, we do not bother to listen. In fact, we do not even recognize that our question may have been answered. Nevertheless, in many cases we look to others to give us answers to questions we have within ourselves. I once heard a story about a man who was running full speed ahead until he fell off of a cliff. He had not realized that there was a cliff because he failed to acknowledge the warning signs. He got caught on a branch, however, and while barely hanging on, he asked, "Is anybody out there?"

"Yes, can I help you?" a mysterious voice replied.

"Who are you?" asked the man.

The mysterious voice replied, "I am God".

Feeling some sense of relief, the man asked, "Can you please help me?"

God said, "Sure, let go!"

The man hesitated for a moment and then asked, "Is there anyone else out there?"

When people do not give us the answers we want to hear, we look in other directions. In fact, even should the answer come from God, if it is not the answer we want to hear, we ignore it as if we had heard nothing at all. The moral is simply: if we choose not to have faith, we can live to regret that decision.

The difficult part of recognizing an answer is accepting it for what it is instead of what we think it should be. Also, just because we have the answer does not necessarily mean that the solution is simple. We may actually have to change who we are or what we do in order for this answer to become a reality. We will have to work to achieve what we are trying to accomplish.

People want great results with no hard work, and actually, there is no crime in that. It may simply be human. We want the riches, but we do not necessarily want to pound the pavement. We may want to be an excellent athlete, but we do not want to practice. We want to be a size 7-8, but we do not want to give up the chocolate candy bars. We know the answer to achieve our goals, but we do not want to do the work it takes to reach them. Sometimes, this very concept seems so simple that we do not recognize that we have a solution. We would rather discover the alternative to facing the challenge by hoping for what are mostly absurd outcomes, such things as somehow inheriting lots of money and becoming rich. What are the chances of that happening? I do believe in the types of blessings that come along and surprise us, but in most cases and for most people, opportunity will only knock if you put yourself in its way. If you did receive this type of blessing though, do not question it. Never question a blessing and never leave one blessing to go in search of another one. Open your eyes and see it for what it is. Accept it and be grateful.

However, you must be sure to keep an open mind so that you receive your blessings in life. Sometimes, you may not recognize that something that has happened to you was a blessing until much later. If you have a closed heart, hand, or mind, you may lose absolutely nothing, but you will not gain anything either. If you do not let love out of your heart, love will not be allowed to enter — and the same principle holds for money and knowledge. If you do not share what you know, what more do you learn? If you do not open your hand to give money, it will not be open to receive it.

Most of us have the amazing ability to see others clearly and as completely as one can see another, along with their faults and weaknesses, but we can't manage to see our own. I believe that we were put here to rely on our fellow man or woman because other people help us to see ourselves in the true vision. So many different people were placed on this earth to do so many different things, and we all have our own set of experiences. If we were not meant to share our challenges as well as good times with someone else, we would all have of the same experiences. In short, life is meant to be shared with others. Others may indeed keep us from expanding our opportunities if we let them, but there are also others who encourage us to live. Those who are happy for you are the ones who are also being blessed, shared with, and advised.

When you have something and you are afraid for others to know about the strategies you used to get it, you will keep that something but you will not necessarily get anything more. It is my goal to be blessed with abundance, and that means that I must give in the same capacity. As long as I give to others and with good intentions, I know that I will be blessed. To me, being able to pour out life's lessons is a blessing. As long as someone has been encouraged to do one thing differently or inspired to find their passion in life, I will continue to be blessed.

I have been a firm believer in this simple concept: if you continue to do the same things you have been doing, you will continue to get what you have gotten and you will continue to be where you have been. I was forced to acknowledge the realities of my experiences when someone shared this insight with me. If you expect to advance, but you have not advanced in a way that you would like, you have to change something about the way that you do what you are doing. One change may or may not make all of the difference, but even one thing different changes your circumstances, and together many small changes added together can add up to a new life.

I know that in life it is a lot easier to say things than it is to do them. The key is that we have to start with something, and saying what you want is the easiest start yet. If you do not know what you want well enough to speak it, how will you get it? In fact, sometimes the hardest part of the process is speaking what you want. Most of us can tell you what we do not want easily, as if it were the memory of something that happened yesterday; but ask us what we do want, which is like asking us to foretell something that will happen in the future, and our response, after telling you what we do not want again, will be to ask what you mean specifically. If you can not answer the question — What do I want? — let me be the one to introduce you to a person who will not achieve their goal, yourself.

Exercise
Accept Change

On a sheet of paper, draw a line down the center. Label one side "Things I would like to change" and label the opposite side, "Reasons why I have not changed".

1. List 5 things you would like to change along with the reasons why you feel you have not yet changed these things.

2. Once you have done this, write a brief paragraph on each topic explaining the steps you need to take in order to make these changes.

3. Once you have written the paragraphs, pick one word to describe how you feel after successfully making each change.

5

School and Education

*Never stop educating yourself. Education leads
to exposure which leads to new experiences.
There is always something more to learn in life
whether it be from books or from others. Create
an educational foundation so that you reap the
benefits of unlimited knowledge.*

First and foremost, let me share with you that I am an advocate for higher education. I do not believe that there is anything better to do after graduating high school than to go on to college or some other type of training, but that is not to say that there are no viable alternatives. One could rush into the work world, getting a fulltime job just after high school with no further education, but we could pretty much predict where this person might be in five years. Most would be wondering where the previous five years went because, after all, time flies. The thing to remember, though, is that we can never regain the time that we have lost. A young person who decides to work instead of furthering his or her education may not get the opportunity to be exposed to so many different people or experiences that support a successful future.

If a teen's parent has been grooming them for the family business or something, then that is a different story altogether, but I would advise such a person to go to college as well so that he or she can acquire the tools to improve even that business. Do not get me wrong, some people will do well in any situation, but the majority would find that there are benefits to continuing their education and would wish that they had explored other options.

Those who choose some form of post-secondary education, however, would be graduating after that same amount of time, four to five years, after learning a lot about themselves and other people, after learning about the types of opportunities that exist for them out in the world, after learning what it takes to achieve success. They may not have chosen a career or be on the path that they desire, but they will be educated and they will have been exposed to much that they would not have experienced otherwise. I guarantee that most of these young people will take something away from their higher-education experience from which to learn and grow on in real life, which is what education is about.

When I was just 17 years old, I was excited about leaving home. I was not sure what my major would be or which direction I wanted to go in, but I knew that my success would begin in college. I started as an undeclared major, but two years later, and after some research, I decided to choose the Sociology program. I was successful, graduating after two more years, but I found myself wondering what I would do with my life now. I was 21 and ready for the world, or so I thought. I spent some time trying to find the right job for me, and after not being so successful in that quest, I decided that I still had more work to do — so back to school I went. I applied to a Master's program, and it was there that I began to discover who I was, who I am. I felt that it was a perfect fit for me, for my personality, and I was validated. After graduating a short two years later, at 24 years old, I was ready to fly.

A few years after my journey in college had begun, I had a close friend who decided to give college a try; but after her first year, she decided it was not for her. She did not really try to fit into the program and thought that she needed some time to figure some things out in her life. She ended up moving in with her boyfriend, even though she was unsure whether that was the right decision.

Within three years, she had decided that this was not the life that she wanted to lead. She also learned that her student loans were in default, that it was hard to find a decent job, and that a boyfriend taking care of her was not her idea of success. She struggled to make ends meet, experienced personal problems as we all do as young adults, and became depressed. One year after that, she realized that she should have stuck it out in college because she would have been graduating by that time. Of course, college does not guarantee a problem-free or trouble-free life, but you do have the opportunity to grow through those changes while you are working towards discovering who you are as well as towards some sort of career.

College is not about the theoretical knowledge, the information that you learn from a book, but about the heuristic knowledge you acquire, what you learn from others' past actions or experiences. After graduating from a university, one has learned what it means to persevere. You have worked to overcome some adversity while still managing to reach your goals. It takes drive and determination to succeed in college, and in many cases, this is the first real test of your endurance.

Graduating from college is a gift, one that encourages the freedom to dream. This gift gives you the freedom to obtain economic independence and the freedom for social advancement, which determines your future. Each of us has the opportunity to become educated, and regardless of your socio-economic status and no matter what neighborhood you are from, an education promises the benefits that a college degree affords, which ultimately means the chance for upward mobility.

We all know that going to college does not guarantee a good, high paying job, but it certainly increases the chances that you will obtain one and is, therefore, worth the risk. We all take chances everyday, because after all, he who risks nothing, does nothing, has nothing, and is nothing. I once had a conversation with a young man who told me that a college degree was nothing more than a tool to get money. Ultimately, a college degree means progress, but it means an opportunity to obtain a higher status in society too. It means being closer to the American Dream.

I had another close friend who always knew that she would go to a university. Before graduating high school though, she had an unexpected, life altering experience. She became pregnant. She was able to finish high school and decided to move in with her boyfriend. She had a beautiful baby girl and picked up where she left off about one year later at a community college. This young woman was now taking on the responsibility of motherhood, which is by far the most extremely difficult and important job one can undertake, while being a fulltime student, working two part time jobs, and eventually becoming a wife. As you could imagine, she carried a tremendous load.

Being a young mother in a marriage, with what turned out to be an abusive man, brought on its share of hard times as well. My friend went from one job to another, had to take a semester off from school on a few occasions, but finally, after 7 years, she graduated from a university to reach her goal of becoming a high school teacher. I watched her go through so much more than anyone should have to experience, overcoming so many obstacles, and fighting to prove that she is strong and will be successful.

My friend is very special to me, and her story proves that, if you have faith and are determined, you can accomplish your goals. Before having a child, my friend shared with me that she had planned to go to college to have a better life and to make an impact in society; but after her daughter was born, she needed to prove to herself that she could do it and show her daughter that she could do it as well. Although my friend has a story of triumph, when asked if she would advise her students to follow her path, she replied, "Definitely Not!" Her advice to high school students is to set your goals early, make plans, and do not allow any situation or person deter you from reaching them. My friend made it through; however, she acknowledges that life could have been so much easier and is grateful for the blessings along the way, whatever it was that allowed her to succeed.

There is absolutely nothing more important than becoming educated, and in fact, education should not stop after obtaining a degree. I remember learning that the smartest person in the world knows how much they do not know. Life offers each of us an opportunity to increase our pool of knowledge, so be sure you take advantage of the opportunity.

EXERCISE
Rate Your Education

Draw one line down the middle of a sheet of paper from top to bottom. Go about half of the way down on the left side and draw a second line all the way across creating four quadrants.

A. In the upper, left quadrant, write down your highest education level obtained. Under this, write down your desired level of education.

B. In the upper, right quadrant, answer the following question:

What were at least 3 of the most important things that you learned while in school? (secondary/post secondary)

C. In the lower, left quadrant, answer the following question:

What are at least 3 new things that you have learned since finishing school?

D. In the lower, right quadrant, answer the following questions:

Did you learn more useful information while you were in school than you have since you have been out?

Would you benefit from going back to school?

Why or why not?

After filling in each of the quadrants, describe the differences between what you have learned in school versus what you have learned since being out?

you or they are not, and whether or not you have their respect will be based upon what you demand from them. It has always been important to me to hold myself in high regard. I always thought that the kind of young man that I am attracted to likes a woman who is confident and smart and who takes care of her business. The key to that last statement was that this would be the kind of man that I was attracted to in return. It never made much sense to me to be the prettiest girl in school with a D average. To be the complete package was always the goal for me.

Let me talk about the complete package from my point of view. To be beautiful, smart, outgoing, confident, and ambitious are attributes that produce quality. A tremendous woman knows what she wants and what makes her happy so that she is able to help her family to find these things for themselves. I am talking about the kind of woman who is strong yet sensitive, smart yet open to learning more at every turn. However, there are so many great qualities that make for a wonderful person, and each woman should be able to define these things for herself before holding herself to another's standards. So spend some time and determine which qualities are important to you.

Many of us are always talking about what it is that we want, but we never think about where we are. If you are expressing a desire to have your "King" or your perfect man, for example, you should be well suited to have "King." I worked hard in my life to be the complete package. I never wanted a man, or anyone else for that matter, to have a reason to complain about something that I was lacking. I wanted to prevail over the competition. I have always felt that I should be beautiful and confident, smart and outgoing, strong and sensitive, to the best of my ability anyway.

You must recognize that, if you have not yet become a "Queen" or that perfect woman, then you should at least be accepting of a man who has not yet become a "King." We all have work to do. I am not saying that you should not desire a perfect man, but that you should be accepting of a work in progress if that is where you are yourself. In other words, have realistic expectations. If you understand what I am saying, then you acknowledge that you should be working on yourself so that you are a "Queen" fit for your "King" when he is delivered to you and vice versa.

When it comes to being a woman, make sure that you believe in yourself. Your idea of what a woman is will be affected by all of the women that you know. Recognize those things that you like and respect in other women and acknowledge them in yourself, but more importantly, be true to who you are and what makes you feel special. I know that there are a lot of societal pressures associated with being a woman, but whatever happens, make sure that you do what makes you feel good. You must be aware, however, that what feels good to you may not always be the acceptable things as far as others are concerned. For example, maybe you like holey jeans and t-shirts because they are comfortable and cute. If this is the case, by all means, wear them. When you make decisions that you feel good about, you are confident and you feel proud of yourself—and this is part of the package.

As far as the education process goes, not everyone is good at academics, and that is okay. However, being smart does not necessarily mean getting straight A's in school, but it does mean working hard. Being a smart person has to do with being able to present yourself respectfully and intelligently. You do not have to know everything there is to know, but you do have to know what it takes to get the information you need. You do not have to know everything about math and English, for example, to know how to make math and English work for you. Being smart means having common sense and using it, and it also means taking the initiative to use what talents you do have, making them work for you.

It is amazing that the rules in relationships do not really change too much. When I was young, my father told me that it was not a good idea to be the intercessor for my friends, to talk to boys for those who may not have the nerve to speak for themselves, or to even pass letters for them, because the boy would end up liking me instead. What are you to do when something like this does happen: your friend's object of affection likes you and your friend thinks that you had something to do with it? The reality is that you showed initiative, personality, and a willingness to be his friend. Oh yeah, one more key thing is that you had no problem looking silly in front of him since you are not the one who likes him.

Kindergarten through fifth grade, what did we know about relationships? The answer is *a lot of the same things we know now.* The players and the game may change, but the rules stay the same, from childhood to the grave. When we grow up, we still find that these young men will be more impressed by a young woman's charm, personality, and willingness to look silly than the girl who would rather stay behind the scenes. Outgoing, friendly, and confident women catch the attention of men.

Speaking of confidence, women must possess this quality, especially if you plan to be in a successful relationship. Confidence does not mean that you know all of the answers, but it does mean that you believe that you can get them. Women often have problems with their physical characteristics, which usually leads to lower confidence levels, but if there is something about you that you do not like, work on it or learn to live with it. If you are not willing to do either, do not complain. I have never been excited about the size of my breasts. They started to grow in about the sixth grade and just did not seem to continue. I have never grown bigger than I was in about the seventh grade as far as my breasts are concerned, but I am still a very proud and beautiful young woman. You see, there is nothing that I can do about my natural breasts, but I can work on other things. For example, I could get a PhD, work out, build a strong mind, and love all of my other qualities. In the big picture, the other qualities far outweigh small breasts. As I always say, you cannot have it all.

I was one of those young women who thought that I would NEVER find a lifetime love. I could never get the guys that I really liked to have the same feelings for me. The truth of the matter is that those qualities that I had been working so hard to possess were not important to the young men in my circle. The guys that I liked were not looking for a wife, and it seemed that I would go from one bad pick to another. However, before college was all over though, I found my soul mate.

It took three years of drama with the man who captured my heart before our hearts would finally meet. There was a lot of love between us, but we were not at the same place in our lives at the same time. He was busy doing what young men do, while I was ready to make the relationship work. He did not want to be committed to anyone, and I could not understand why. I always thought that we had a special connection, but I would tell myself that he probably had that same connection with other young ladies he was seeing. After having my heart broken so many times, I tried to accept just being friends with this young man and asked him to let me be. He ignored me every time I made the request, however, ringing my phone again after just a few weeks and sometimes after a few days. It is so hard to say no when your heart says yes.

Just before graduating from college, all of the things that I had done to improve the quality of our relationship had begun to become apparent. I always thought that it was important to be sincere in an attempt to be his friend. I truly cared about his well-being and his happiness, and I wanted him to recognize that fact. I wanted him to know that I cared enough to be there with him through the trying times, and unlike some of those with whom he had involved himself, I would always have something to offer. By this time, he had recognized all of those things and our relationship had grown tremendously.

After finally choosing to give in to the love that we each felt, I asked him why he had finally decided to pick me. He admitted to me that I was by far the best pick because I had been working on myself as well as being there for him. I cared about his future, whether or not I was a part of it. I continued my education to assure that I would reach my career goals in life, but I was also concerned with helping him to sharpen his skills so that he would have a fulfilling career. I spent time building my resume while helping him with his. I was genuinely interested in his life, his past, and recognized what an accomplishment it was for him to have achieved what he had achieved at that point in his life. I was also very honest about who I really was and what my dreams and passions were. I was not concerned about what he could do for me more than I cared about what I could offer him.

The truth of the matter for me was that he made me feel. With him, I felt a connection, a bond and I knew that it was special. You never really know if any relationship will last these days, but together, you and your partner have to have faith, you have to believe.

It is not enough to hook your mate; you have to reel them in as well. Once you have found a partner in your life, you both need to work hard to assure happiness for the two of you, and the only way to do this is to communicate with one another and to be honest. Every person should be honest about their needs as well as their desires if they want the relationship to work. If you are content with the lifestyle you have, living in a nice apartment and working a nine to five for example, but your partner is aspiring to live in a mansion and start a family business, then the two of you are going to have problems. It is my belief that life mates should inspire and motivate one another to achieve, but you have to have similar goals because they will indeed affect your lives together.

It becomes very important as we get older that we are able to be honest with ourselves about our desires so that we are able to share this with our partners. If you expect to meet your ultimate goals in life, if you expect to live your dreams, you must share these things with the person you have decided to share the rest of your world with. If you ever find that you are embarrassed to share the things that you want in life with your partner, then you have a few issues to work on in your relationship. Your partner should be your primary source of support if you expect to have a lasting and fulfilling relationship. If you find that you have a need to prove to your partner that you can reach your goals because you do not feel that they believe in you, you may begin to shut them out—and this certainly means that you have some reevaluating to do.

You have to work really hard in a relationship to see to it that you are both meeting each other's needs as well as expressing your own needs to your partner. No one I know reads minds all that well. The most important thing in a relationship, as has been said time and time again, is communication, but more importantly, you need honest communication. Do not get caught up in telling your partner what you think they want to hear, because ultimately, you will be unfulfilled. It would really be terrible if you found that the person you were sharing your life with was not sharing their true feelings with you because they wanted to say the things that you wanted to hear. What a waste of time.

It sometimes takes a little longer than we plan to meet our passions in life. The reality is that most of us spend so much time working toward what other people want for us that we never stop to think about whether we are doing what makes us happy. Often our parents may see in us a certain career field or position, for example, and maybe we have gone through an educational system that promises a certain type of lifestyle if we follow the right path. But if you have found that the track you are on is not the one that will bring you ultimate happiness, even if you have been working towards this for years, you should realize what it is that you need to do to find your passion.

In a relationship, it is essential to share with your partner your desires as well as your fears. You should not feel afraid to be honest about who you are, and you should never feel as if you are in competition with your partner. However, you also need to recognize that it is okay to be in a position that is unfamiliar. Changing your life's journey or expressing feelings of uncertainty are normal feelings. If you have not quite had a chance to discover what it is that you want out of life because you have been busy worrying about everyone else, the feelings of fear and anxiety that go along with this path are also very natural feelings. There is a lot to be said for a person who decides to start a new journey in life, in the quest for ultimate happiness. Each of us has a passion, and it is up to us to work towards finding it. If you plan to be in a fulfilling relationship, encourage and support your partner to do the same thing. Maybe you two will find that your passions meet, allowing you to work together in order to meet your goals together. Remember: being in a relationship is all about compromise.

Exercise
The Love You Create

Think about your ideal relationship. Draw a circle in the middle of a sheet of paper and inside of the circle, write "My Ideal Partner".

- Draw a line that extends from the outside of the circle outward. At the end of the line, write a word or phrase that comes to mind when you think about your ideal partner in a relationship. Put a small circle around that word or phrase and continue doing this for about 5 minutes or until you run out of words to write. When you stop, it should look like a cluster.

- Once you finish, write a brief paragraph summarizing your cluster. This should take no more than 5 minutes.

- If you are in a relationship, compare your situation to that described in your cluster.

7

WORK AND BUSINESS

In the workplace, make decisions that allow you to feel accomplished and appreciated. Be creative and find something about your job that you enjoy, or change your circumstances into ones that work for you. Remember that no relationship is one way and that there should be reciprocation.

L ife presents us with an opportunity on a daily basis, the chance to start anew. Tomorrow, we will see things that we did not see today, if we open our eyes and focus in new directions. Many of us graduate from high school and go on to college expecting amazing things to happen, but if you are anything like the average student in college, you have no idea what you are going to do in any specific way after graduation. We select majors based on what we think we know about certain occupations, and we learn the skills it takes to do the job.

Being a highly skilled employee is a great thing, as long as that job meets your needs. Some people are lucky enough to find good jobs early on, but sometimes they end up being the ones who spend years in a place that does not challenge, enlighten, excite, or support them. Work and what we do for a living is such an integral part of who we are that each of us needs to be sure that our needs are being met. If you are the type of person who enjoys traveling, for example, you should have a job that at the very least accommodates you with vacation time.

Along with the opportunity to do something new daily, each of us also has the chance to see new places and different things. Sometimes a change of atmosphere is all we need for a fresh start. Regardless of whether you move to a new place or not, however, you will still be the same person. So the goal is to address any issues before you make any major changes. Be sure that you are making the right moves for the right reasons.

New places have always been exciting for me. When I started out in the workforce, I always looked for an opportunity to master my job. It was important for me to do well and to learn all that I could. My intention as an employee was to do my job and whatever else I could do to help to make things easier for me, the department, and the company. I think that most employers appreciate having employees with this kind of attitude. These individuals are usually self-starters and highly motivated, and they are often the type who believe in doing things for themselves. As an employee, I worked hard and I expected to be rewarded for my hard work. Reward for me was recognition, appreciation, and a nice salary, to name a few things.

Personally, from the time I started my first full-time job, I knew that I would need to make a difference, be significant, help others, and be successful. I also learned very early on that if I could not get to a place where I was really happy, I would not be doing any given job for long. Life offers too much for me to accept the minimum, which was sitting in traffic for an hour, going to a job that offered no personal satisfaction, and working for someone who does nothing other than tell me what to do, while the best part of my day (which went by too fast) was my lunch hour, which I spent in the car, wondering why I felt like a loser, only to wind up back in traffic for another hour to get home to a wasted day. That is not living. The fact that some people do this for 20 years seems insane to me.

Experiences like this landed me back in school. I still was not sure what I was going to do with my life, but I knew there was something that I needed to pay attention to, and that something was my personal fulfillment. I needed to do something that meant success to me, something that allowed me to help make a difference in other people's lives, something where-in my passion would be appreciated. As I mentioned before, my Master's program was one that I fit into naturally. I enjoyed going to class, the discussions, and the activities—and it was at this time that I learned the most about people. It was also a time that I learned a lot about myself. Self-fulfillment does not come without knowing yourself.

I have had several jobs that allowed me to help others and to reach a personal level of satisfaction. As we grow, our ideas and our desires change, and this was the case for me as well. In fact, I expect this kind of change to continue. You cannot let fear keep you from doing what makes you feel good, and changing jobs or moving to a new place are a few of things that sometimes make the difference. It is always important to weigh the options to your happi-ness, your needs versus your wants. I have weighed my personal satisfaction against the size of my income on a few occasions and learned that I needed to take the steps necessary to change my situation. I have never made one of these very major decisions without seriously listening to my inner being. It had to feel right, even if that meant I was not sure how I was going to pay the rent in two months. There was still plenty of opportunity to make something happen in the meantime.

One of the most challenging situations I ever had to face was making the decision between necessity and desire just after graduating from college. Every new college graduate has dreams of finding the perfect job, a job that will allow them to feel a sense of purpose, of satisfaction. I was also searching for that dream.

When I started going to the university, I wanted a job that was flexible and not too demanding so that I could focus on my academics. I was lucky enough to find the ideal job for my situation, but three years later, it was time to find something with more responsibilities. I needed some professional experience, more work hours, more job duties, and more money. Not long after I had come to this conclusion and started my search, I found a suitable job. With only two semesters left of school, I had begun to focus my attention on my career, my future.

A co-worker brought up the idea of continuing on with the same company and advancing to another position, which having my degree would allow me to do. Until that point, I had not even considered such a simple solution. I could skip all of the hassles of looking for a job and stay on where I was. Well, with all of the worries that go along with being a senior in college and maintaining my grade point average, having an internship, and having a job, I welcomed the opportunity to stay on and train for a new position with the company that I was working for at that time.

I graduated, and immediately the new position was postponed. They needed me to fill in for someone who had recently left the company. I was glad to help out in the beginning, but my feelings of self-worth had quickly begun to diminish. I felt as though I was not being appreciated, and I did not like it, but I knew I had to remain patient. After a few months, I was at my limit, but I needed my job because I was my only source of financial support. The new position as a Marketing Representative was finally offered to me and I gladly accepted. My excitement wore down quickly though. After all, it was the same company that I had come to understand the dynamics of a long time ago.

Two months had passed, and something was still missing. Each day I wondered how long it would take or what it would take to fill me with the satisfaction I was longing for. Deep down, I knew that I would not be with the company long because it was not where my heart was. I wanted to help people, make a difference in someone's life, but at the time, I had to provide for myself. The question became one of necessity or desire. Working fulltime made it difficult to actively search for a more fulfilling job, but the longer I was there, the more work experience I gained. It was not too much longer before I made my move, however. I knew what I had to do if I wanted to be happy. Before finding a new, more meaningful job, I put in two weeks' notice. I had taken the first step towards my happiness, and I did so with great pride. Desire was the ultimate choice, and it was then that I began my journey working in education, starting off as a substitute teacher. Although a part of me had no idea what I was going to do next, I was filled with gratification and relief.

It is extremely important to consider the consequences of the choices we make. Something may seem easy or less stressful at the time, but that does not mean that it will remain that way. I certainly learned that the easiest choice is usually not the best one. I took a chance to improve my situation, and I realized that, before money or status, my happiness depended on the fulfillment of my desires. I will help others until life's end because that is what I was put here to do. Even though I had to make a drastic decision, I knew that it was the right one because it felt right.

I have left employment before and never missed anything other than the paycheck. I remember talking to my father once about how I felt insignificant at my job, and his response was that it was the employer's job to make me feel that way. I understood that to mean that, as long as I was not fully motivated or as long as I did not believe in myself, I would remain a faithful employee and not venture out or take chances. It was a valid consideration in my life at the time and has made all of the difference. I learned not to be afraid to listen to myself. I would be the perfect employee for any employer, but what I wanted was more important, and that was to be fulfilled. It is sometimes tough to make these important decisions, but I had to weigh the options and start to live for me, not my employer. My life has not been the same since.

I also had another very challenging work experience. After being in an environment where my skills were quickly acknowledged, I found it hard to accept that I was also being envied, especially when it came from the ones I tried my best to support. I have always been very organized and creative, and therefore, when things were missing, I created them. I was not afraid to ask for what I wanted, and that also seemed to cause a lot of jealousy amongst my coworkers because so many were overworked and underpaid. I not only knew what I wanted, but I had the skills, knowledge, and nerve to get it.

In many cases, I felt badly for those people who had been working at this company, because they allowed themselves to become content. Most of them were no longer motivated and were quite unhappy as a result. Therefore, they did the minimum. I watched them get beat down by an unappreciative, manipulative, dictator-style boss. I stayed with the company for a short time, and my time there was truly a blessing in disguise. I learned a lot, although it was one of the most disheartening experiences I have had and turned out to be very negative for me. But surviving this place was also one of the most challenging things that I have ever had to confront. Something positive can be gained from every negative experience, and this one certainly ended with positive results for me.

Sometimes in life we experience precipitating events that change our world. This brief time period in my life led to tremendous change. Sometimes, when things go wrong, it is a sign that new situations need to be considered, that new ideas need to be explored. I could have wound up a miserable and unmotivated worker for someone who did not recognize my value or appreciate my worth. I had to step out on faith, take a stand, and I reaped the benefits. From this job, I started a career in the field of real estate, initially as a loan officer and later becoming a broker. Being a broker allowed me to start my own company and experience the freedoms associated with being a business owner.

Before leaving my job, I purchased a four unit apartment building with my significant other, and our real estate broker was one of the least knowledgeable people in real estate. Honestly, this man did not know a lot, to say the least, and dealing with him led me to understand that, if he could do this, anyone could. I took my chances, and although becoming a real estate broker changed my life for good, the true benefit in real estate is owning it. Leaving my job and starting this new career in real estate introduced me to a reality that I had not known. My viewpoint in regard to managing a company and leading staff was shaped by my personal experience working for a boss who did not appreciate hers. It is my belief that you get positive results when you have a positive work environment. This is true for employees or employers.

Sometimes, when things do not work out the

way you plan, it may just be that there were some other options for you to consider that you may not have recognized otherwise, and this is true for every negative situation. Again, choose to grow from your experiences and they become blessings.

Exercise
Work for Yourself

Rank the following job related items in order of importance from 1-20. (1-most important)

_____ Vacation Time

_____ Personally Rewarding

_____ Opportunity for Growth

_____ Supportive Environment

_____ Competent Upper Management

_____ Training Available

_____ Requires Travel

_____ Salary

_____ Retirement Plan

_____ Benefits (ex. Medical, Dental, etc.)

_____ Educational Reimbursement Plan

_____ Close to Home/Commute Time

_____ Flex-Schedules (ex. longer day, shorter week)

_____ Overtime Available

_____ Team Oriented

_____ Diverse Environment

_____ Receptive to Change

_____ Location (ex. near shopping)

_____ Extra-Curricular Activities

_____ Access to Technology

ၓ

Money and Credit

*Develop a comfort level with your desire to have
or not to have lots of money. Be honest about your
financial picture so that you can make improvements
that are measurable. Determine your financial goals
and educate yourself on reaching them. Your credit
profile is an extension of you so take good care of it.*

It has been said that money makes the world go
around, and depending on whom you ask, it can
also turn it inside out and upside down. Each of
us knows that money is essential when it comes to living a successful life, and while many know what to do
to be financially secure, or at least stable, many more
do not.

In this book, I talk a lot about taking the steps to
finding your ultimate happiness and reaching your

passion, but I am sure that many people have not been able to do this thus far in life for fear that their passion may not support their lifestyles. Sometimes, it is simply that the risks are too great. Many people are forced into a way of life because we all need money to survive. Some have taken steps to secure a position with a company that pays them enough to support themselves and their families. Others have convinced themselves that they need more money to improve their lifestyles. Those people either work harder and longer so that they might get that much needed pay increase or they look for better paying jobs. Some people work overtime, take on a second job, or go back to school to improve their chances of getting a higher paying job. All of these things are viable options, but be certain about which sacrifice you can truly afford to make. Before taking any major steps that will inevitably take up more of your personal or family time, be sure to seriously consider the alternatives.

If money, or the lack thereof, is or has been a problem for you or someone that you know, take a moment to fully examine your true financial picture. In order to make any changes in life, including those to your financial status, each of us has to know our starting point so that we recognize progress. When it comes to money, so many people never truly eval-uate where they are financially because many are afraid to know the truth. If it turns out that you are overspending, for example, you may have to give up something that you really enjoy if you truly want to improve your financial situation. Making a lot of money but having nothing to show for it is hard to accept. I recall watching a television show where a scenario was presented about a young woman who spent nearly $400 per month on a special brand of coffee but had tons of credit card debt. While she may have never looked at the coffee as a big deal, she was paying the minimum payment on a credit card, which had a $400 balance and was accruing interest, and spending $400 on coffee with nothing to show for it. Most of us would agree that it was time to give up the coffee, or to at least cut back until that $400 credit card balance was paid off. In order to change this picture, she would have to give up something she really likes, coffee.

A financial education is extremely valuable to have in life, but most people are never educated in this way. Our school system does not educate us about money, and unless we have a parent, family member, or another financially successful adult to teach us, we typically learn through experience. I can remember being in school and learning everything there was to know about math, subjects like algebra and geometry, and I must say that I can not ever remember using any of it in real life, other than maybe showing a younger person how to do a math assignment. I was taught nothing more about money than how to write amounts correctly. However, I use money almost every single day. Now, how does that make sense if it makes any sense at all? The inevitable thing is that children with no financial education become adults without it.

When the subject of money comes up, credit is never too far behind. Understanding credit and how it works is usually another area of wild misinterpretation. Many adults do not grasp how credit truly works until they are over their heads in debt. We are taught that credit is an alternative to money for getting something that we want or need. The bulk of what most people know about the subject, however, is that you can use your credit card when you do not have cash available and pay them back later.

When I went on to college, I learned this by way of experience. I acquired a few credit cards and was quite comfortable with paying the minimum balance. Although I did not know much about how they worked, I knew that I did not like the idea of owing people. I did not want to ruin my credit so that a creditor never had any reason to deny me. I watched my friends go shopping, putting shoes, handbags, designer jeans and more on credit cards, acquiring more debt than they knew what to do with. I did acquire some debt in college, but because I was cautious, I was never in way over my head. It was not until I graduated from graduate school that I began to understand the significance of having a quality financial profile.

In working with several people on their credit

situations, I have learned that many people believe that credit card companies are actually helping them out or doing them a favor. While in many cases it may be helpful that you are able to buy groceries or pay an important bill on a credit card, never forget that there is a price for everything and that credit card companies are in business to make money, just like any other business. Sure they are increasing your limit and allowing you to pay a minimum balance, but they also benefit when you take advantage of their offers. Do not buy in to the idea that they are primarily helping you. You make their business.

When people do not understand how credit works, they spend and spend and overspend, paying the minimum monthly payment allowed. Sometimes, there may be a small amount due, like $15 for example, and people do not think that this amount is crucial so they might skip a payment or two and double up on the next one. Actions like these are the worst things you could do for your credit profile.

Speaking of credit profiles, each of us has one even if we have no idea what it looks like. We are evaluated against a number scale (also called a FICO score) that rates our credit worthiness from 300 to 850. We are rated according to how many credit cards or accounts we have along with the balances and limits. We are rated on how long the accounts have been open, how many times we have been 30, 60, or 90 days late making a payment, and on how many accounts we have neglected or refused to pay, to name a few criteria. The more late payments you have on your record and the more credit cards you have with high balances, for example, the lower your FICO score will be. The goal is to have the highest FICO score possible to achieve the greatest benefit from credit, which amounts to more than simply credit cards. We need credit for several important things like renting an apartment or buying a house, buying or leasing cars, mobile phones and more. It is especially important to understand how credit cards work so that you can avoid getting in over your head, but it is also absolutely important to be credit worthy in a capitalistic society.

There is nothing wrong with wanting nice things, and there is nothing wrong with having nice things either, but be smart about how you get those things. Evaluate where you are now financially versus where you would like to be. If there is a gap between the two, then there is work to do. Discover your starting point, or where you are today, and then write down your monthly income on a piece of paper. Beneath that, make a list of your monthly bills. Be sure to include entertainment, things like going out to lunch, dinner or a movie. If you are having trouble coming up with a list, get a copy of your most recent bank statement or checkbook register and write a list of all of the checks that you have written, including ATM charges, and categorize them according to type of expenses. Once you have done this, you will be able to look closely at how much money you bring in each month versus how much money goes out, which gives you a better understanding of your true financial standing. If you find that your expenses exceed your income and that you have no savings, you are setting yourself up for financial disaster unless you change this picture. Be honest with yourself, but please note that you are far from alone if you are in this position.

Money affects relationships with loved ones. In fact, money has been recorded as the top reason many marriages end in divorce. Money has been called the root of all evil, after all, but it does not seem that many take this to heart. People are considered successful based upon how much money they have, and failures if they have none. Money is a symbol of status. Money determines what kind of lifestyle each of us will have, and financial education dictates how long we will manage that lifestyle. There is nothing wrong with wanting money, and there is nothing wrong with having money.

I used to feel guilty about wanting too much because we live in a society that generalizes about having just enough for the important things in life and endeavors to convey that money is not everything. I would think about other people who may be less fortunate and remind myself not to ask for too much. Today, I think much differently. I want others to have all that their hearts desire, and I do not feel guilty about improving my financial standing. In fact, it is my goal. Life can be a joy with or without money; however, if you expect to get money, you have to deal with it openly. I once read the following analogy: if you pile sand into the palm of your hand and close it, squeezing too tightly will cause you to lose most of the sand. The same concept applies to money. Do not hold on to it too tightly. Although you may not lose any, you will not gain any either. Deal with money with an open hand so that there will always be room to receive it.

Make smart decisions in life regarding how you make money and how you spend it. Work smart so that you are able to experience life's rewards. Live below your means and be sure to treat yourself, but be sure that the treat does not cost you too much in the end. Seek advice from others who have money, and maintain the type of lifestyle that you aspire to have while doing so within your means. Learn as much as you can about how money works and about credit choices, and if you are not willing to change anything in your life to improve your financial status, do not complain about where you are and just be happy.

As I have said before, life is for living with abundance. Take the time to pull your credit profile so that you can find out your FICO score. If you have any debt, be sure to be responsible about making your payments, and only use credit cards when you really need to. Save money and learn the difference between assets and liabilities. Not all things that appear to be assets are. If something takes money out of your pocket instead of putting money in, it is a liability. Learn how to buy assets to cover your liabilities. If you need to take a major step to improve your financial status, do so, but be sure you understand what you need to do to get the results you truly want.

Money is important and so is credit. Money ties in to almost every area in life, so please get educated about money and live the life that you want to live.

EXERCISE
Your Financial Picture

Develop an individual financial plan.

- For this activity, you will need your most recent month's pay stubs (two if paid bi-weekly). If you have a partner who contributes to the household income, please get their information as well. You may also need your check register or your current bank statements or bills.

- Write your net monthly income at the top of a sheet of paper. Next, make a list of all of your monthly expenses, including fixed and variable. Estimate an average amount spent on variable expenses and be sure to include entertainment. Once you finish this list, total your expenses and subtract it from your monthly income. Write down the amount of money you have left after expenses.

- Once you look over this list, create a chart of *Action Items* in order to change your financial picture, if you are not satisfied with your situation.

- On the chart, create a Action column, a column for your Current Standing, an After the Change column, and a column for the Difference the changes will make.

- Repeat this exercise over a few months to see how much you are actually spending. Revisit the chart in 3 to 6 months, depending on your situation, to measure your progress.

3rd

PART OF THE PLAN

9

FEED YOUR SPIRIT

*Regardless of the path that you are on presently
or the one that you have been on, close your eyes and
go to that place that your spirit takes you. Feel what
your spirit moves you to feel and develop an opportunity in your life to find that place regularly.*

It is not always clear why things happen in life, but
it is up to each of us to discover what those reasons
are for us. Many people have given up on the
challenge of seeking true happiness for themselves.
The truth of the matter is that it is much easier to go
with the flow and let life happen. For example, if you
are interested in running your own business and you
do the proper research, you will discover that it takes
a lot to run any business if you expect to succeed.
The responsibility involved may be more than you

are willing to deal with, which means that you have other, more important priorities—and that is okay.

There is nothing wrong with prioritizing. In fact, I recommend that each person do this several times in his or her adult life: check, or re-check as the case may be, what your priorities are by making a list. The reality is that your priorities will change, and this is perfectly normal. If they do not change, then it is a sign that there has not been much growth for you, and that is a problem. There is too much to discover out in the world for there to be no significant changes in your life. Each of us as individuals have the freedom to choose if we want to act on those changes or not, but that is different than recognizing the change in the first place.

On some days, I have found myself ignoring the urge to get out there and take on those things that are important to me. I have also found myself struggling to understand why that lack of motivation has existed in my life. I am motivated and extremely driven, but even I have those days where I seem to be paralyzed. I sometimes sit back and take it all in, and the only thing that moves me is another soul in need of my guidance or support.

I recognize when I am in need of guidance, however, and it comes from the spirit. When I have not been fed spiritually, I seek understanding in my life. I know that we all get hung up sometimes where we just cannot seem to move forward, and it is at these times that I am reminded to ask for that nurturance. Nurturance comes in many forms, and for me it starts with faith.

At times in my life, I found myself with all of the things that made me happy. I wanted to be in a different place in my life as far as my career goes, and I had started to do what it took to get there, but for some reason, I could not rest. I was down and I did not understand why. My soul mate would ask me what was wrong, and I even asked that question to myself, but I could not answer that question. I had begun to evaluate my life, and I was bothered by the fact that I was missing something. It amazes me that, even if everything in your life is working, if you are not fulfilled in your spirit you can see nothing but gloom. I recognize that my spirit needs to remain healthy, and to accomplish spiritual health, the spiritual body needs to be worked out, just like the body does if we are to be physically healthy.

For me, the spiritual body workout is up to the spirit. If you do not know what it is, think about that thing that makes you feel good, that thing that makes you exhale. It may be reading a book or watching a good movie. It may be talking to a good friend or going out with your soul mate. You may have a method that works for you, like prayer, and there is indeed power in prayer. It may be a nice warm bath with candlelight and a sweet aroma so that you have a moment to think with no one else around. It may even be going to church. Whatever it may be, be sure to recognize that your spirit is growing with love when you feed it.

Exercise
Remember Your Spirit

Build a poster of happiness. You will need poster paper, tape, and some pictures of yourself.

- Take a look through some of your photo albums. Find 5-10 pictures of yourself while doing an activity that you really enjoy or while being at a place you really enjoy being. Tape these pictures to a small to medium sized poster board and underneath each picture, write a small caption of what were doing or where you were. Above the picture, write one word that describes how you felt at the time the picture was taken. Be creative and hang this poster in a place that you visit often.

- This "Poster of Happiness" will serve as a reminder of some of your happiest times and will encourage you to revisit activities that will help to feed your spirit.

thought that he knew everything and that he was the smartest man in the world. The craziest thing was that my opinion mattered to him, and that felt good. I did not think that my encouragement of my father to strive to do better or to expand would make a difference, but I have learned otherwise.

I have also used that same encouragement to support my soul mate. I have encouraged my brother, my uncle, and my cousins, all of whom have reached a crossroads at some point in their lives. It never occurred to me that, just as I love to dream and just as I have made major decisions to change the direction of my life, so have they. I always see myself making the most difference for those who are like me, but I have learned that all *people* have people problems.

With every move I make in my life, I believe that I am getting closer and closer to my destiny. Nothing, and no one, can stop you from achieving great success the way you can stop yourself. I have been my greatest critic, but I have also been aware of my strengths. It is true that I have wanted to be perfect, but I also know that one of the first things we learn in life is that no one is perfect. No matter how good something or someone is, there will always be something or someone better. With this in mind, it amazes me that people will let perfection be the reason they do not move ahead.

Every time you try something new and it does

not work out, you will have learned what not to do or you will be that much closer to that thing that you are supposed to be doing. I tried and failed in several business attempts, and I believe that each time this happened has led me closer to doing the right thing. That right thing will be that place where my heart rests. If you are the type of individual who wants to be an entrepreneur, for example, and you discover an idea that you think will be successful, you should try it. If it does not work out, it will lead you closer to that other idea that you should try until you get to that place. Maybe it is in the location of your business, or maybe the type of business that you start will introduce you to another while you are developing it and lead you to another path. I have learned about occupations that I never knew existed by way of another business idea that I had that did not work out.

Think about what will happen if you start a business that works out. You are earning the money that you hoped you would. You are meeting the type of people who are supportive and successful as well. You have a great staff and you utilize or believe in your own product. If this turns out to be the case and you find that you are happy, most people will stop looking and recognize their blessing. You would have to be very unclear about what it is that you want if you found that you were still searching to reach your goals in business.

Once you have acknowledged that you've made

her, and I found myself explaining that she was a slave who escaped to freedom and returned to lead other slaves to freedom on the Underground Railroad. It never occurred to me that any American adult would not know who Harriet Tubman was, regardless of their race or background, but I learned a very valuable lesson that encouraged me to continue on my journey toward writing this book. Many of us have a lot of experiences and knowledge to share with others, so keep in mind that not everyone knows what you know.

EXERCISE
Now and Then

Draw 2 lines, separating your sheet of paper into thirds.
Compare your life 5 years ago with your life today and
list your goals for 5 years from now.

- Label the first column, "Where I Was 5 Years
  Ago". Under this column, write down the things
  that you were doing in your life 5 years ago
  including things like where you lived, what your
  job was, how much money you were making and
  so on. Write a least one major goal you wanted to
  accomplish.

- Under the second column labeled, "Where I Am
  Today", describe your current situation. Keep in
  mind the questions you answered in the first column so that you can compare the two columns.

- The third column should be labeled, "Where I
  Am Going". Under this column, list your 5 year
  goals for the categories you visited in the previous
  columns. Be sure to write down the things that
  you need to do to reach these goals.

- Set realistic deadlines for yourself and feel free to
  add to or change your list of goals as your life
  changes.

11

REACH YOUR PASSION

While reflecting on your experiences, never stop reaching for your passion. Life is about reaching your passion, and each of us has to figure out that thing that we have been put here to do.

This is my formula for reaching your passion, and it usually starts with the end in mind. The beginning of the process is to think about what you want in your life as opposed to your current situation. Once you are able to visualize and verbalize what it is that you want, whether it is realistic or not, your attention is captured by that desire. Because something seems more like a dream than reality does not mean that it is not possible, and in fact, if you want something badly enough, it becomes a dream. After being able to clarify what it is that you

one book. I have also gone to seminars, ordered audio tapes and programs that will assist me in the process of writing a book and understanding how to make the most profit possible off of my own creativity and abilities. I have written my goals, including an objective, determined who my target audience will be, decided how much money I would like to earn, outlined several topics of importance to me, and I have come up with a plan to make writing a book happen in a minimal amount of time.

I have everything that I need in place to take action. I started with the end in mind: I want to write a book. I then outlined a few very important reasons why I would like to write a book, and I became motivated by those reasons. I saw myself as an author and speaker, and I started to speak it: I will become a best-selling author and inspirational speaker. I got excited about the reality of this vision, this plan. What can possibly stand in the way of me reaching my goals? What do I need to do to make it happen? I drew up an outline and did the research, and now it seems real. I want it, and I know what I need to do to make it happen. I have all of the materials that I need, and now it is time to get it, to reach the goal.

I started writing as often as something would come to mind, even before I had become driven. However, I found myself stuck for a while and not really sure why this rather somber feeling had taken over. I was motivated, and I knew what it was that I wanted. I was not sure how to get it, but I wanted to write anyway. I continued looking for things to write about, and I would go over and over what I had written looking for inspiration. The truth of the matter was that my discomfort, my stuckness, was not due to my lack of actual motivation but in the drive, the action. What did I need to do to become driven? I needed to look beyond my desires, and even beyond motivation, at how to make my dreams into a reality. And I needed to look at how this accomplishment would make me feel. I needed to take action, and until people know which way to go they will sit still. I was still until I found the drive, and now I am off on the road to reaching those things that I am passionate about: writing this book to inspire you to reach your passion, expressing myself, exploring my creativity, and setting myself up on a path to become wealthy by doing what I love. I am ready to tell the world about it.

One last, very important factor that makes this process work is FAITH. I believe in God and I believe in me.

Exercise
Identify Your Passions

Finish the following sentences.

1. My hear pounds with excitement when I…

2. I feel especially proud of myself when I…

3. I get a lump in my throat when I…

4. Tears of joy come to my eyes whenever…

5. I lose track of time whenever I am…

6. When I dream about my future, I see myself…

7. If I could live anywhere in the world, I would choose…

8. If I could change one thing about the world, it would be…

9. When I was a child, I always liked to…

10. If I were independently wealthy, I would…

12

Happiest Day

On the happiest day in my life, everyone around me, especially my loved ones, would be happy. We would all recognize what we need to change in life in order to grow. We would reach goals we never expected to reach. We would believe wholeheartedly in a God who works for us. We would not be jealous. We would believe in ourselves as well as work to uplift each other. We would dream as well as follow our hearts. We would acknowledge any wrongdoing in our lives and work to make things right. We would give love and we would have love in our lives. We would have money and an abundance of joy. If I had my way, each of us would be in this place right now.

It would certainly be a lot to ask to hold off on my own happiness until others see the light, and I realize this. However, the dream does not stop me from trying to do just that. Realistically, I would be delighted if I could be instrumental in helping others to come to this place in their own lives, but the truth of the matter is that I can only work towards God's vision for me. I want others to reach their ultimate happiness, to feel accomplished, but everyone has to make that determination on their own, what happiness means for them and how to achieve it.

In recognition of my dream, I offer this book to you, full of life lessons. I have included examples of real life situations from my personal experiences or from those that I know. This book is my effort to help you reach your goals, to share with you what I know to be true. I am attempting to show you how I have applied these simple rules in my own life or better yet, why I believe these lessons to be essential for personal growth. I have experienced the good and the bad and I expect that I will experience many more good and bad times however, I know that I am blessed to acknowledge real life lessons from either of my circumstances. I believe in opportunity and this was my opportunity to make a difference to someone, even if it is just one. Sharing my experiences with you makes me happy therefore I know that I am working toward doing my job. My hope is that you will allow yourselves to open up and acknowledge your own life lessons so that you too may share them with another.

Take a moment to review the life lessons that I offer in this book. These lessons are meant to help you recognize what might be a lesson in your own life. They will assist you with making the changes necessary to improve your situation or help you to make a difference for someone else. Many of these life lessons have been emphasized at the beginning of previous chapters and although all have not, each point has been made throughout the book and should be considered for a successful transition.

• In life, be sure that you take the time to get to know yourself. No other person is more important for you to acknowledge and understand than you. Acknowledge those experiences in life, the good and the bad, that have made you into the person you are so that you will recognize progress and growth.

• Regardless of the path that you are on presently or the one that you have been on, close your eyes and go to that place that your spirit takes you. Feel what your spirit moves you to feel and develop an opportunity in your life to find that place regularly.

• No matter what decisions you make in life, be sure to acknowledge that God has a vision for you, and no matter how hard you work on creating your own, God's plan for your life will reign supreme. Spend your time trying to align your vision with God's, and the only way to do that is to be at peace with your spirit. You must believe in and love yourself, which comes as you begin to love that peace felt when your spirit guides you.

• Always recognize that life is change, and that

therefore you should not be afraid of it. Change is growth and expansion. Change is freedom and accomplishment. Life is all of these things, and therefore change is life.

• Be sure to fill your life with love. No one has life without love. We will never run out of love to give to others. Love comes from an infinite source, and our lives are meant to be filled with it. The more you love, the more love you will receive. The more you share love with another, the more that they may share with someone else. Do not be afraid to love, and start off by practicing on yourself. Learn about yourself and love yourself despite the things that you may not like about yourself. Once you are able to accept the things that you cannot change and change the things that you can, you will begin to lead a happier, more loving life. Once you are able to love yourself despite your shortcomings and mistakes, you will be able to love another despite theirs. Allow yourself to love instead of working so hard against it, and you will be loved more.

• Always remember to seek happiness in all areas of your life. Be sure to evaluate how you spend most of your time, and do all that is possible to be happy in that place. Work hard to find happiness and stay there. There is no place more beautiful.

•Never stop educating yourself. Education leads to exposure which leads to new experiences. There is always something more to learn in life whether it be from books or from others. Create an educational foundation so that you reap the benefits of unlimited knowledge.

• In the workplace, make decisions that allow you to feel accomplished and appreciated. Be creative and find something about your job that you enjoy, or change your circumstances into ones that work for you. Remember that no relationship is one way and that there should be reciprocation.

• Determine the most important things in your life and prosper. Go out and get the things that you want. Achieve your goals with great pride. No one can stand in your way without your permission, and no one can stay in your way like you, yourself, can.

• Never give up on your dreams, and always believe in your ability to achieve personal success. Be sure to evaluate yourself because only you can develop the criteria for your peace of mind.

• Make moves until you get it right, no matter how many times it takes. Life was not given to us so that we would be miserable.

• Develop a comfort level with your desire to have or not to have lots of money. Be honest about your financial picture so that you can make improvements that are measurable. Determine your financial goals and educate yourself on reaching them. Your credit profile is an extension of you so take good care of it.

• Accept that some days are going to be exciting and that others will be more somber. Spend as much time as possible enjoying all your days, but acknowledge when you are being given the time to reflect.

• While reflecting on your experiences, never stop reaching for your passion. Life is about reaching your passion, and each of us has to figure out that thing that we have been put here to do.

• Determine what makes you tick, what gets you going and work to get it, to achieve that goal. Believe that you can have it and that you deserve it and it is yours.

• Never stop working towards your own personal success. Remember, only you can determine what that is.

Upon reviewing these life lessons, many of you will recognize that you have had the solution to a problem that you have been facing all along. You probably remember a time that you shared one of these lessons with another but forgot about the lesson when your problems clouded your own view. Solutions come from within us. Although many of you have struggled with making the best decision when confronted by one problem or another, you can acknowledge that you knew what you needed to do but you were afraid to listen to your spirit. Recognize your life lessons and accept your decisions as the best ones to make at the time. Be honest with yourself, have faith and do not be afraid. Even if the decision turns out not to be the best one, there is a lesson of growth in it.

We are not expected to make the best decisions all of the time; however, we should be able to live with the decisions we make. In order to do so, think about the things that are important to you in life, your goals, and determine if the decisions that you are making will affect the likelihood of you reaching those goals. Life is about expansion. Your success is determined by you. Accept change as a natural part of life, like growth. Live to change and change to live. Put yourself in the way of opportunities and don't put it off another day.

Special Thanks
...Because I Want Them to Know

Over the past few years, I have come to a very special realization in my life and I must give thanks to a few people who inspired me in ways they do not know.

First, **Lauryn Hill** awakened me to an awareness in my life that I had not known. Your music introduced my heart to my spirit and I have to thank you for that. It was not just your words but your voice that empowered me and not just your confidence but your fearlessness that made me proud. Your music opened up my heart to God from where I was. Thank you.

India.Arie came to my spirit at the perfect time. Your music is a guide to happiness that supports a calming, inspirational, yet expansive journey. You said exactly what I felt only I had never heard it before. Your music is an extension of my connection to God, assuring me that I have both recognized something special enough to hold on to, but also motivating me to share it with the world. Your music speaks to my heart and my spirit. Thank you.

Oprah Winfrey has reinforced that the key to my dreams begin and end with me. You are phenomenal, your vision incredible. You are an inspiration to an entire culture of people and you are a blessing to so many. You have given me a goal beyond the stars and you are definitely my idol. Thank you.

With Absolute Sincerity,
Na'Kisha

Na'Kisha Crawford is an accomplished **Author,** professional **Life Coach** and **Inspirational Speaker** whose goal is to inspire you to Experience the Journey.

"I encourage you to **Dream Big; Open Your Heart; Always Have Faith; and Follow Your Spirit** *Towards Ultimate Happiness.* I work to be a positive influence, stimulating you to inhale and realize your greater purpose in life, your greatest potential."

"Individuals have individual dreams and talents. If you want to improve the quality of your game, it is best to get a coach. They see you where are you are and they give you the tools necessary to reach your personal best."

—Na'Kisha Crawford, M.Ed.

If you are interested in getting more information on life coaching or for a complementary coaching session, please visit us at www.nakishacrawford.com .

For Speaking Engagements or Author Appearances or if you have any comments or feedback on this book, please visit our website at www.nakishacrawford.com

AUTHOR

N a'Kisha Crawford has spoken to thousands of people from various backgrounds on topics ranging from basic counseling skills to personal and professional growth and development. She has been fortunate enough to work with people from a variety of social, economic, and ethnic backgrounds which has provided her with an understanding of the unique yet similar needs of people. Na'Kisha earned a Bachelor of Arts Degree in Sociology as well as a Master's Degree in Education, Counseling from San Jose State University. Upon the turn of the new millennium, Na'Kisha was the brainchild of the first pageant, Miss Positive Pathways Pageant, dedicated to increasing the awareness of positive thinking and presentation, conducting workshops on positive self-esteem and positive self-images for young women.

Na'Kisha has participated on a variety of panels addressing issues related to successful college transitioning as well as those that have emphasized women in higher education and non-traditional professions. She has facilitated individual and group counseling sessions in addition to workshops on developing effective counseling techniques. Na'Kisha has lectured collegiate level courses as well as written and implemented lesson plans for high school students on various subjects. These experiences have provided her with critical knowledge about the recruitment and retention of underrepresented communities in higher education.

Na'Kisha is a licensed Real Estate Broker and loan consultant and she is also co-founder of a real estate and investment firm, serving as a corporate officer and CEO. She has consulted for small businesses, helping to create procedures, forms, and even promotional packages. She has created and coordinated training manuals and materials and she has also developed and designed internship programs.

Na'Kisha has written several articles and her debut book, "I Want It Now" has taken the literary world by storm. Na'Kisha is confident that her professional and educational experiences support her qualification. She was born a life coach and she has a strong interest in the educational development of aspiring students. Na'Kisha has a genuine desire to help people achieve ultimate happiness and success in life. She is a natural leader, she is experienced and she is professional.

At the young age of 27, just days before one of the most special days in her life, Na'Kisha was diagnosed with Breast Cancer. She embraced this as the most challenging process she would encounter being faithful that wonderful things were to come for her. She held her head up gracefully and accepted this challenge. Na'Kisha is now Cancer Free and she is sharing her passion with the world. She has an energy and an excitement that we cannot afford to miss. She lives in Southern California but she is ready for the world.

To send to a friend or to order individual copies of *I Want It Now!*, please send a check or money order for $13.95 + $3.00 shipping and handling to:

Pathway Publishing
9849 Foothill Blvd. Suite A
Rancho Cucamonga, CA 91730

Be sure to include the following information:
Name
Return Address
City, State, Zip
Country

Discounts may be available for bulk purchases.

For more information or to order online please visit our website at:
www.nakishacrawford.com